Copyright © 2023 Pearl Robinson

All rights reserved. No part of this publication may be reproduced, distributed, or transmitted in any form or by any means without the prior written permission of the publisher, except in the case of brief quotations embodied in critical reviews and certain other noncommercial uses permitted by copyright law.
Printed in the United States of America

Introduction

This book teaches children that it is okay to love sports; Children will learn that playing sports means someone loses and someone wins. But, when they trust Jesus, everyone is a winner. It also teaches children to obey their parents because God commands this and that telling other children that Jesus loves them is okay.

Jamel put on his favorite black and white shorts and a jersey outfit. His jersey had the number 11. He washed his face and brushed his teeth. Then he went to breakfast.

Jamel sat at the table, waiting for his mother to give him his favorite cereal and a glass of orange juice. He loves orange juice because his father said it would give him energy. Jamel's mother asked him whether he had put away the toys he played with. He replied. "Yes, Ma'am!"

Jamel sat on the chair in the living room, waiting for his friend Dustin to come over. He was ready to play basketball. Looking out the window, he saw Dustin walking up the sidewalk to his house.

Jamel grabbed his basketball and met Dustin in the front yard. They walked to the basketball court. Dustin wore his red and black outfit. His jersey had the number 3 on it. After talking for a while, they were ready to play, both eager to win.

They continued playing. Jamel shot the ball and scored. Now the game was on.

Jamel scored again as Dustin watched in disbelief. Jamel had a look of excitement as he played his favorite game.

After a while, they sat on the bench and drank water. Jamel's parents told him to drink water when he plays. He always listened and obeyed his parents because he knew this was what God said to do.

After the game, they sat, talked, and drank more water. Dustin wasn't upset because he had won the last game, and he and Jamel were best friends. They didn't let basketball come between their relationship.

He sat down with them and asked who won. Jamel replied, "I did!" Then he asked Dustin how he felt about not winning. Dustin replied, "I'm good," I won the last time we played." Jamel and Dustin understood that in sports, someone wins, and someone loses. However, in the end, they were still best friends.

As Dustin was about to leave, Jamel's dad told them that in basketball, some lose, and some win. He told them that Jesus loves the winner and the one who loses. He also told them everyone is a winner when they know and trust Jesus, who died on the cross and arose on the third day.

They stood up; Dustin hugged Jamel's father and thanked him for sharing Jesus's love. Then Dustin leaves.

While back in the house, Jamel sat on the couch with his father and mother. Jamel asked his father why he shared the story about Jesus because he already knew. His father replied, "I wanted to make sure Dustin knew." He told Jamel that God wants all to know about His son and His love for everyone. He said, "We must always be on fire for Jesus, sharing His love to all."

Jamel learned that God wants all to know about His son Jesus. He was happy and proud of his father. Jamel's mother asks, "Who wants to watch a movie?" Everyone agreed, and they sat on the couch, eating popcorn, candy while watching a movie and laughing.

After watching a few movies, it was time to eat dinner. Jamel's mother left to prepare dinner. Jamel and his father joined her in the kitchen to eat. She had cooked Jamel's favorite food, mac and cheese, fried chicken, and corn.

After dinner, Jamel was tired. He went to his room and got ready for bed. He prayed and laid down. Jamel has a red and black basketball pillow his mother bought him. He laid down on the pillow and fell fast asleep.

THE END

About The Author

Pearl Robinson is a wife, mother, grandmother, and great-grandmother. She has an unbridled passion for teaching children. She taught Sunday school for children and led the Children's Ministry in her church for many years. She believes that the best gift one can give children is to teach them about the grace and knowledge of Jesus and lead them to accept Jesus' gift of salvation while they are young. Pearl writes from her heart because of her love for God and His people. She is truly a God-inspired writer.

Printed in the USA
CPSIA information can be obtained
at www.ICGtesting.com
LVHW062007260324
775532LV00005B/188